The Peter Pan Alphabet

The Peter Pan
Alphabet

OLIVER
HERFORD

with pictures by THE AUTHOR

Serenity
Publishers, LLC

ROCKVILLE, MARYLAND

2016

ISBN: 978-1-61242-874-1

Published by Serenity Publishers
An Arc Manor Company
P. O. Box 10339
Rockville, MD 20849-0339
www.SerenityPublishers.com

Printed in the United States of America/United Kingdom

A ROUND ROBIN
TO
J. M. BARRIE

From His Humble and Devoted Servants

THE ALPHABET

The Lord forgive if we transgress
Thus to familiarly address
    One of our betters.
But Jamie, do you no recall
The slate whereon you learned to scrawl
    Your Humble Letters?

Well we remember how you drew
Our shapely features all askew,
    Unflattering really.
You made A lame and B too fat
And C too curly—what of that!
    We loved you dearly.

From that first day we owned your spell,
And just because you used us well
    We served you blindly.
Why, even when you put us through
A fearsome Scottish Reel, we knew
    You meant it kindly.

Jamie, 'tis said Grand Tales there be
Still biding in the A B C—
    If this be true, Quick Jamie!
Cast your golden net.
Maybe we have the grandest yet
    In store for you.

Contents

A is for Adams 11

B stands for the Boys 13

C is the Crocodile 15

D is for DoodleDoo 17

E is the Exit 19

F is the Fight 21

G is Old Glory 23

H stands for Hook 25

I's for the Indian Girl 27

J is for John 29

K stands for a Kiss 21

L is the Lion 33

M is for Michael 35

N is for Napoleon and Nana 37

O's for Odds-fish!! 39

P is for Peter 41

Q is the Quiver 43

R's for the Redskins 45

S is the Shadow 47

T is for Tinker Bell 49

U is the Underground Home 51

V is the Verse 53

W's Wolves 55

X is the X Ray 57

Y is for Youth 59

Z is the Zebra 61

The Peter Pan

Alphabet

A is for Adams

So **A** is for Adams, Oh! fortunate A
Luck certainly seems to be coming your way.
In the Days of my Infancy, A I recall
Stood for Ant or for Apple or anything small.
Now A stands for Adams, Maude Adams, Hurray!
I always *said* A would be Famous some day.

B stands for the Boys

B's for the **B**oys, all as **B**usy as **B**ees
They are building a Little House under the Trees
With funny red walls and mossy green roof
Where Wendy may live from danger aloof.

C is the Crocodile

C is the Crocodile Creepy who ate
The right hand of Hook and covets its mate
He makes a loud ticking wherever he goes
For he swallowed a Clock (To kill time I suppose).

D is for DoodleDoo

D is the Dire and Dread DoodleDoo
With which Peter Daunted the Pirate crew,
And demolished a foolish old Proverb for good
By crowing before he was out of the wood.

E is the Exit

E is the Exit the three children made
With Peter and Tinker for guides, Who's afraid?
They sailed through the window as calm as could be
Like three little Cherubim out for a Spree.

F is the Fight

F is the Fight, Peter Fought unafraid
And F is his Falchion (Poetic for Blade)
And F's the Fine Feeling all Fearless Boys Feel
When they give a Fierce Pirate a taste of Cold Steel.

G is Old Glory

G is Old **G**lory—that Peter upreared,

When Hook in the Crocodile's
smile disappeared,

And the Decks were still wet with the terrible stains

Of *Invisible* **G***ore* from the Pirate's veins.

H stands for Hook

H

I'm sorry for **H**, tho'
I don't call **H**ook mean
For wanting to Blow Up his own Magazine.
I've known a Good Author blow up, in a **H**uff,
A Magazine just for not printing his Stuff.

I's for the **I**ndian Girl

Peter Pan was too coy for the **I**ndian Miss;
She sighed for his scalp—all she got was a kiss.

J is for John

J is for John (No, he hasn't a Pain;
He is Red-Handed Jack of the Pirate Main).

K stands for a Kiss?
Oh, stern featured **K**!
Who would have suspected—*You'd* leanings that way!
Peter called *his* a Thimble—(*I* think it sounds tame
To call **K**isses Thimbles—but what's in a Name!)

L is the Lion

L is the Lion who lashed his Fierce Tail,
And did Peter Tremble? did Peter turn Pale?
Not Much! 'Twas the Lion who moved to adjourn,
He couldn't turn Tail, Peter left none to Turn.

M is for Michael

M is for Michael—ssssh!—whisper it low!
In Pirate Circles he's called Blackbeard Joe!

N is Napoleon—Mystic—Profound
And N is for Nana the Noble Nurse Hound—
Two wonderful natures—each great in his way, One's
dead and the other is "Having his Day."

O's for Odds-fish!!

O's for Odds-fish—the Pirate's Oath.
To print such a word, Gentle Reader, I'm loth.
And should *You* be guilty of language so low,
I should have to stop calling you "Gentle," you know.

P is for Peter

P is for Peter, and so are we all,

May he ever keep young and his Shadow stay Small.

Yet I think 'tis a pity the White House is Bann'd.

As President, Peter would simply be Grand!

Q is the Quiver

Q is the Quiver from which Tootles drew
The Arrow that nearly pierced poor Wendy through.
'Twas Peter's *Kiss Button* that stopped it—Ah me!
If Kisses *were* Buttons—how *safe* they would be!

R's for the Redskins,
who Guarded the Cave.

What a Treat to see "Injuns" sit up and Behave!

S is the Shadow

S is the Shadow—tho' not of much use,
You'd surely be Sorry if *Yours* Should get loose.
So See to your Shadow—be sure it's on tight,
When Peter lost *his* he was in a sad plight.

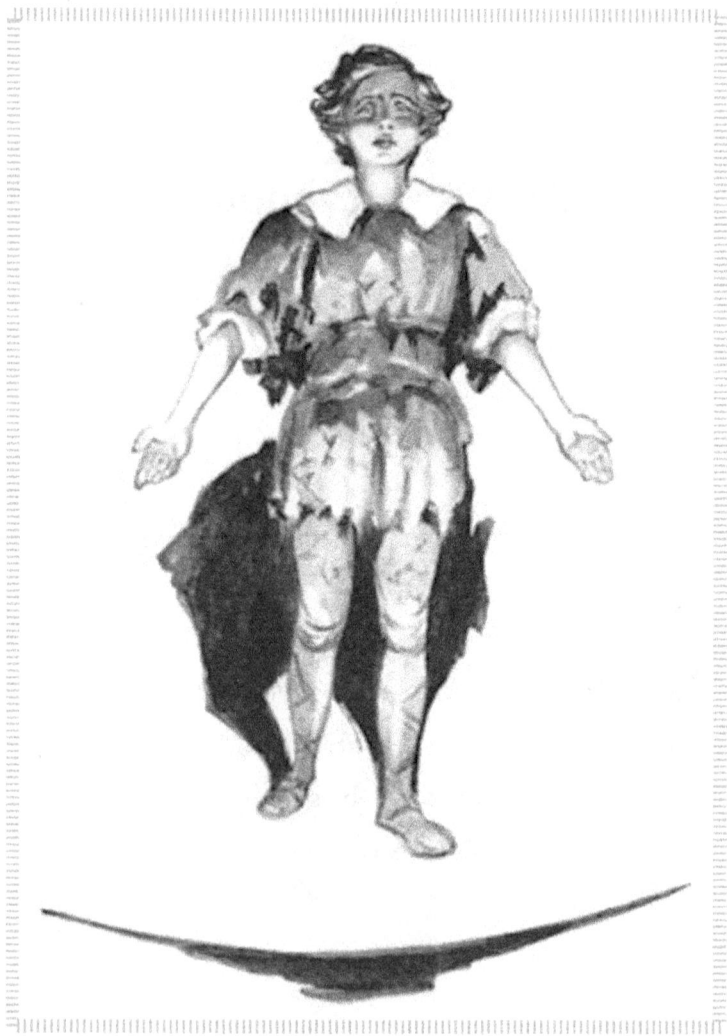

48

T is for Tinker Bell

Poor Tinker Bell's dying, Quick! say you Believe
In Fairies, that Tinker New Life may receive.

U is the Underground Home

U's the Underground home mid the roots
of the trees,
Where when not slaying Pirates,
the boys take their ease.
While Wendy sits mending their shirtwaists and hose,
And the Redskins above Keep watch against foes.

V is the Verse

V's the Vile Verse that the Pirate Bawled—
It was not his language so much that appalled,
Nor the Tune—nor his Voice which was
    Raucus and Deep
'Twas *the way that he sang it* That made your flesh creep.

W's Wolves

W's **W**olves—'Tis said they will fly
If you look through your legs at them straight
    in the eye.
That's how the Boys did it, but if I were you,
I'd experiment first on a wolf in the Zoo.

X is the X Ray

X is the X Ray by whose light alone,
This last fleeting picture of Hook may be shown.

Y is for Youth

Y is for *Youth* to which Peter clung,

But where is the land where he learned
to Stay Young?

Ask Peter, he'll tell you, Geography scorning,

"Second Turn to the Right and keep straight
on till Morning."

Z is the Zebra

Z is the Zebra the Boys *didn't* meet,
But without which no Alphabet's really complete.